Ping and His Chickens and World War 2

AuthorHouse™
1663 Liberty Drive
Bloomington, IN 47403
www.authorhouse.com
Phone: 1 (800) 839-8640

Published by AuthorHouse 10/15/2018

ISBN: 978-1-5462-6399-9 (sc)
ISBN: 978-1-5462-6400-2 (e)

Library of Congress Control Number: 2018912281

Print information available on the last page.

This book is printed on acid-free paper.

authorHOUSE®

Ping and His Chickens
and
World War 2

PHIL VERNON

My home in the Philippines

We lived in Dumaguete, a small coastal city on Negros Island in the Philippines, which is about 300 miles south of Luzon, the major island. It was 1951, and I was 11 years old, having been born right before the Japanese invaded the Philippines. To avoid the Japanese, our family escaped to New York City to wait out the war (See the 2nd section of book).

We returned to Dumaguete in 1946 so my dad and mom could continue their missionary work at Silliman University where my father, Douglas Vernon, was Presbyterian Church Minister. Our return to Dumaguete took some adjustment for me. It was so different from the hustle and bustle of Riverside Drive in Manhattan, New York City, where we lived in an apartment complex for missionaries on furlough.

My dad didn't have a middle name, just Douglas Vernon. I had a middle name. I was named after Philip Harwood Vernon who was my great great grandfather. Although I had _4 this big name, I was called Ping by our servants Liling and Simuna. In our part of the Philippines, children's nick names often were made by taking the 1st letter of the 1st name (P) and adding "ing" to get Ping. They never called me anything else; but not my friends, they wouldn't dare.

Mom's name was Dorotha, but her friends called her Dot. To me this seemed like a silly nickname, but she didn't seem to mind.

Mountain Vacation

I'm awake and I can hear kitchen sounds. Liling and Simuna are starting to pack for our trip into the mountains. I had been sick for over 6 months, mono or some other condition. Our family doctor told my parents fresh air and rest might do me some good. I packed my clothes, a couple of layers in prep for cool mountain air. I felt OK, just never good; and I was tired all the time. I was OK with our trip into the mountains, although the trip meant time away from my friends, and I would have to entertain myself.

The mountain group included Mom and I, Liling and Simuna and our 2 drivers. Dad was staying home to handle his church work. My older brother Hugh was in boarding school.

Liling and Simuna were patient with me, Mom would get a Little testy. She was concerned I was becoming a spoiled brat. True, I demanded attention, and when I wanted something I did all I could to get it.

I recall one time when I spotted a little figure hanging from a Christmas tree branch. After closer inspection, I was looking at a toy soldier; just what I needed to command my troops outside in the bushes. I was pulling the soldier off the branch when Mom saw me..."What are you doing?"

"I want to play with him."

"No, Phil, he's a tree ornament, I've had him for years, you know that, keep him on the branch."

That did it. I started to cry, first I primed the pump, then I was into a full-out brawl. My brother, home for Christmas vacation, heard the commotion and walked out of his room. He had a scowl on his face. He had watched this fight of wills many times, you know he wanted Mom to win. For me no turning back. Crying so hard, my face became beet red and I sputtered, gasped for breath.

Mom stiffly took the soldier from the branch, handed it to me, turned around and left the living room, Hugh retreated into his room. Immediately I stopped crying. I felt no remorse.

My stick figure fighting force was much stronger now. I declared my new toy soldier experienced and a general; you could tell by his uniform. I even assigned him his own security guard. The other side would have to account for leadership skills in attacks. Since I moved both sides, wasn't hard to have the bad guys in full retreat. Stick figures, many shot in the back with rubber bands, falling out of branches, lying in the grass. I made sure to pack my stick men for our time in the mountains.

The Chickens

I was outside watching Liling and Simuna pack when I noticed the 2 chickens, a hen and a rooster, lying in the dirt beside the rice bag, canned goods and other food stuffs, pots, and drinks. I could hear feeble clucks, could see them struggle uncomfortably.

Their legs were tied; I felt sorry for the chickens because I knew chickens were not joining us for their health. Later, they would have their heads chopped off and be defeathered and then placed in a pot for supper, probably some kind of a yummy chicken adobo.

Liling was rough with the chickens. She didn't seem to care about them and threw them into the back of the jeep. They landed with a thud, bound legs thrashing.

The trip took about 3 hours. Our two jeeps took us up the mountain. Trees along the route thrust their branches upward to reach open air as if to avoid the thick underbrush that threatened to cover the road. The road was asphalt to start with and then dirt and then we reached the thatched roof house on stilts we would live in for 2 months. Mom and I had different reactions to this house in the jungle.

The house was up in the air on stilts to keep rain water from seeping in. A tall person would have to bend over to go under the house.

Mom, Lilling and Simuna and our two drivers helped unpack the jeeps. Lilling equipped the kitchen with its wood-burning stove with canned goods, rice bag, soft drinks. Tap water would be boiled, left to cool, and then used as drinking water. Our 2 chickens were kept on dirt floor under the house.

Our small house in the mountains had been very important to us in the past in our escape from the Philippines right before the Japanese invasion.

We settled into mountain living routine. Not feeling well I stayed close to home; I didn't have much to do.

I began thinking about the chickens. I noticed Liling had untied their legs and would give them food and water and some kind of seeds. Before long they were foraging for food around our house. Because of the plentiful food and water, they had no reason to leave, and they stayed below the house.

Every morning the rooster would greet us with the cock-a-doodle-doo. I could tell the chickens felt comfortable around our little house. I started to feed the hen from my hand. At first she was hesitant to approach me, but before long I had the chicken pecking seeds out of my palm. Peck, peck would tickle my palm, make me giggle.

Chicken Little

Soon, the hen was not afraid of me; I worked out a call and every time I made this call she would come running, and I would feed her. Chicken and I developed a special bond. I decided to call her Chicken Little, a name I got from one of my books.

Chicken Little became my pet, my pet chicken. When I would call, Chicken Little would come running, even if it wasn't feeding time. When I came out in the yard Chicken Little would follow me around.

I lost interest in my stick men and war games. Chicken Little entertained me.

I grew to "know" my chicken. I began to train Chicken Little to sit on my shoulder. At first I would pick her up and set her on one of my shoulder blades. I could feel her feet digging into my shoulders as she balanced herself as I walked. I did this repeatedly, and soon Chicken Little would fly up to my shoulder and land safely. I could hear the "whoosh, whoosh," of her wings as she came toward me. Chicken Little couldn't fly far, but she could fly high enough to reach my shoulder or reach a low tree branch where sometimes she would roost at night.

I could tell Chicken Little enjoyed sitting on my shoulder as I walked around, working to keep her balance. She would be perched there even when I took a short hike down our road.

One rainy day, when I couldn't go out to play. I picked up "Little Lootie" one of my favorite illustrated books to read to her. I think Chicken Little enjoyed the vibration and sound my neck and throat made as I uttered the words. She sat very still. I wondered, you don't suppose...no, I didn't think so, still I imagined reading all kinds of books to Chicken Little.

Mom had noticed my reading out loud and how much time I spent with Chicken Little, and how tame she was. Chicken Little had no fear of humans, particularly people she knew.

My mom warned me, "Philip, we can't have your chicken approaching neighbors or flying onto the shoulders of our friends and neighbors. We'll get complaints for sure."

Chicken Little and Her 1st Chick

One day at about supper time, while I was outside leading Chicken Little around, Liling approached me. I was quick to anticipate what she was going to ask, and I said, "Oh no!! We can't have Chicken Little for supper, she's tame and my pet. Besides, I've been watching her, I think she's ready to lay an egg."

Liling... "How do you know that?"

"She's been squatting a lot, looks uncomfortable, her feathers are ruffled, and I think she's made a nest out of dry grass and twigs beneath our house.

"You could be right, your chicken is old enough to lay an egg, could be she had a visit from the rooster."

"Do you mean I could have a baby chick, I mean could Chicken Little have a Baby Chick?"

"Yes, there is a good chance of that. Maybe after she has a few chickens, we could have one of the chicks for supper when they get old enough."

"No no!! I can't imagine eating Chicken Little or any of her chicks. Please, please, promise me. Can't you go to the market and pick up another chicken?"

Liling knew when I made up my mind that was it. I was spoiled from all my mom's attention, and I must say I did take advantage of Liling and Simuna. Some times I would get them to do things Mom had asked me to do. Fortunately, they never squealed on me.

I knew right then I had to keep a hawk eye on Liling. With my experience as a stick figure general, I knew how to recognize the enemy, and to protect the troops. Liling was the cook, and she was going to be a problem with regards to Chicken Little. She looked at a chicken as something that should go into a pot, and unlike me she had no feelings for Chicken Little.

That's How It All Began

Next morning I got up early, ran outside and under the house. Chicken Little was on her nest. I just knew she had laid an egg over night, and was sitting on it. I didn't want to frighten her, but I had to see the egg. So I got some seeds and held out my hand to lure her off the nest. When she hopped off the nest I took a quick look and sure enough, one egg in her nest, I was so excited! I let her return to her nest, and she resumed sitting on her egg.

I ran into the house and woke up Mom, Liling and Simuna.

"Chicken Little is a mother hen!"

I could tell Liling pretended to be excited.

I asked Liling, "How long will it take before I get a chick?"

"Not sure, I think it's about 3 weeks."

"3 weeks! That long!"

"Yes, chick has to grow strong before it can peck its way out of the shell."

Every day for the next 3 weeks I would check out Chicken Little on her nest. She would only leave the nest to get food and water, and before long I placed seeds and water right by her nest.

Liling scoffed, "You don't have to do that. A hen knows how to take care of herself and her egg. She will protect her egg." I could sense Liling's growing impatience.

I began my countdown, and every day I would check on her and make sure she had enough food and water. Day 1 became 2, which became 10. I lost interest in anything else. Chicken Little and I were having a baby chick; that's all that mattered now. I wondered whether

Chicken Little's chick would be born during the day or night. I asked Liling who had about had it with my interest in all things Chicken Little.

"I don't know! When the baby chick is ready to break out of its egg, it will break out!"

The Chick Is Hatched!

Day 21 came, not yet. Shoot! I was so ready. Then on day 22, I rushed out of bed down the stairs and beneath the house, and lo and behold Chicken Little was up and about, close to her nest, and right next to her, a little white and yellow fur ball, the cutest chick I have ever seen. Chick went "peep, peep, peep."

I was so excited, I rushed into the house and woke up Mom, Liling and Simuna. "I have a chick, a baby chick, so cute!"

Mom..."Philip!! It's not 5:00 yet." Liling moaned.

Over the next week or so, as usual Chicken Little would follow me around, who in turn was followed by her chick. I would call to feed Chicken Little, and soon I was feeding the little chick. They were a pair.

Would there be more to come? I asked Liling.

"There's a chance she could lay an egg next month. Once they start, they lay an egg about every month or so."

I thought..."Oh man another wait!" For the next month, I would stay close to the house almost playing the role of an expectant father. We had 2 worlds in our little mountain house. The inside world where Mom, Liling, Simuna, and I lived, and the outside world, with Chicken Little and whatever else was out there. We did our best to keep the outside world out. Our house had no window screens so we slept under mosquito nets. No pets or animals in house. This would soon change, by necessity.

One day I asked Liling an important question, "Is the little chick safe with woods all around the house. I hear lots of animal sounds from the woods."

Lilling..."Well there are jungle rats, lizards, snakes, wild cats. Any one of them would love to get their paws on a baby chick. These wild animals also like to eat chicken eggs."

By the gleam in her eye I could tell she enjoyed telling me this horror story.

By this time Chicken Little had returned to her nest, had laid another egg; her little chick always staying close. In 3 weeks, another....

Then and there I decided I had to move Chicken Little, her nest, egg, and her little chick into the house. I found a good spot against our dining room wall, close to the door to my room.

Next hurdle, I had to ask permission. Mom...I knew better than to ask Liling or Simuna. Liling couldn't care less. I waited until mom seemed to be in a good mood, and then I approached her.

"Mom, I have to move Chicken Little and her nest into the house."

She was distracted, thinking of something else, but she did put together "Chicken" and "into the house." This got her attention.

"What do you mean? We can't have a chicken in the house."

"Liling warned me, something might try to eat the chick and egg. It's dangerous out there near the woods."

"You know it could be real messy. What about her droppings?

"I can housebreak Chicken Little."

"You're kidding me. You're going to housebreak a chicken?"

"Sure, Chicken Little is inclined to go outside anyway, and her Chick always follows her. Feathers...I can clean them up, that shouldn't be a big problem."

"You get to tell Liling and Simuna."

When I mentioned the move to Liling she just stared at me. Would guess she thought I had gone over the edge. I liked the idea of Chicken Little in the house. She did not. I was surprised mom didn't object more to my bringing chickens into the house. We had returned to the Philippines after the war. I was in mountains to convalesce, to gain strength. Perhaps mom thought my caring for chickens would help take my mind off my condition. Even Liling's blank stare on hearing I wanted to bring Chicken Little into the house indicated she could handle letting some outside life in.

That's how it all started. Chicken Little and her little chick lived by my room in our little house. At night she'd climb the stairs followed by her little chick, she would settle down with her chick. Next day she would exit house the same way. She spent most of the time outdoors, I fed and gave her water outside.

Importantly she never messed inside. She must have known she had to go outside, always followed by her chick. As far as Liling was concerned, Chicken Little's life depended on it.

Mom did notice I started looking and feeling much better. Thanks to Chicken

Little, I had a great project that kept me involved day after day.

What really pleased me was when it came to egg laying time, Chicken Little made a nest by my door, bringing in twigs and dry grass. I had created a safe place for nest, and Chicken Little used it, aggravating Liling and Simuna to no end. Winds would blow through the house spreading dry grass around. Liling could never get over having to step around nest, and the chickens. Nest area was definitely off limits. I was excited but nervous. Liling always had a pot in the ready.

Sure enough, a few days later Chicken Little laid her egg in the nest, and she began sitting on it. Whenever anyone got too close, Chicken Little would let them know it. She'd cackle, and ruffle her feathers. I knew to give Chicken Little space during these times. She would protect her egg. Little chick was always around.

Meanwhile Liling was having conniption fits. She had to give nest area a wide berth. Simuna had to sweep up grass and twigs that the wind would spread around. Never in Liling's wildest dreams had she expected to live and work in what had become a hen house.

Before long, I had 3 chickens... Chicken Little and her 2 chicks, 1 newly hatched. When I left house, I led a parade of 3 chickens, walking smartly in formation. All of them had imprinted on me, and they would follow me anywhere. At night Chicken Little would find a resting place in our living room, chicks nestled around her. I couldn't be happier. Liling couldn't be more flustered.

The Secret Life of Chicken Little

A disadvantage of living in the woods/ jungle in the tropics was the multitude of insects and little animals that always were around the house and in the house. Wasn't long before mice found us. I would see them in the kitchen scurrying around looking for food. Mice would often wait until we were in bed before venturing out to find food crumbs. I would see them in our living room and dining room. Liling would walk into kitchen in the morning, and she would clap her hands to "clear the decks." She did not. I repeat, she did not like the mice. She'd put mouse traps out, and most mornings Simuna would dump trapped mice in the woods.

One day while I was sitting in the living room reading a book, I noticed a mouse creeping along the floor near the far wall. I watched the mouse with some interest, after all, these little creatures were driving Liling and us crazy.

Suddenly, BOOM! Chicken Little was on the mouse in an instant. I jumped in surprise, startled by how quickly Chicken Little had pounced. She had mouse by the neck in her beak. WHAM! She began shaking the mouse violently, the mouse screeching in terror. GULP! The mouse was gone, down Chicken Little's throat. No sign of mouse at killing scene except for a few mouse hairs and feathers.

I sat wide-eyed. I just had witnessed one of the most violent acts I had ever seen. Chicken Little turned away and returned to her nest as if nothing had happened. I caught my breath. Man! that was something.

Thus, Chicken Little exposed a side of her I didn't realize existed...for me, a secret life. Before this I had seen Chicken Little only eating seeds. That's all I fed her. I thought she was a vegetarian. I didn't realize she liked mouse meat.

This began her process of clearing all mice from kitchen and living room. She was good... fast and deadly.

Before long we stopped seeing mice and mouse droppings in the living room and kitchen. Simuna put away the mouse traps. As long as Chicken Little was in the house, we would not be bothered by mice. I wondered if mice began boycotting our house to avoid being eaten.

I asked Liling..."Did you know before that chickens are good mouse hunters?

"No. No one ever said anything about it."

I didn't ask, but I doubted if she had changed her mind about Chicken Little in the house. Nevertheless, I was proud of my little hen. She was a predator. If you were a mouse, you'd better give Chicken Little a wide berth or better yet, stay out of the house.

In a whimsical mood, I wondered if I were shrunk down to mouse-size, would Chicken Little spare me? I was glad I never had to find out. I wasn't sure I could trust her; she did such a good job of consuming any mouse she got her beak on.

Return to Home Base

Time came to head down the mountain. I had had a great break; color had returned to my face. I felt good, and I had gained a Chicken family.

One big problem. Our departure date happened to coincide with Chicken Little's egg laying time. It had been 4 weeks since her last egg, so I knew she was due any day.

Drivers arrived to take us down mountain. They helped Liling and Simuna pack the 2 jeeps. With all the hustle and bustle, Chicken Little and her 2 chicks had retreated into the woods. I shouted to our helpers, "We can't leave until Chicken Little lays her egg!"

"Say what?"

"And we have to wait quietly so she will come out of the woods."

Liling was beside herself.

"Better do what Ping says, unless you want to spend the night here."

I had everyone move away from the house, "Shhh." And we waited. One of the men lit a cigarette. And we waited.

I could see Liling who was shaking her head. Would guess she was hoping Chicken Little and her 2 chicks wouldn't show, and we would leave without them.

I fidgeted. I knew Chicken Little would need to lay her egg. Suppose she was too frightened. Suppose she wouldn't return.

I was staring at the spot in the woods where I had seen Chicken Little disappear. It was quiet. Surely, any time. Our temporary neighbors had dropped by to see us off. As asked, they all kept away from the house. And there were Mom and I, Liling and Simuna, and our 2 drivers, waiting in a large semi-circle around the house.

Some probably didn't understand what we were waiting for, or why they were kept away from the house. Jurassic Park like, would we feel ground tremble, hear trees, bushes being crushed? Would we see a huge creature break out of the jungle and move toward us, nostrils blowing smoke?

Nope. Emerging from the jungle was a little hen followed by her 2 chicks. Caught up in this imaginary arrival scene, everyone held their breath.

You could feel the suspense.

"What's going to happen now?"

Chicken Little, followed by her 2 chicks, began walking toward the house. "Shhh," I said. She was in no hurry, walking in that Chicken-way of hers, her head bobbing, 2 chicks right behind. What was missing was the Rocky theme song. I heard a chuckle from the bystanders. Up the steps they went, into the house, to what I was sure was her nest. I doubt if anyone had witnessed such an event before.

"Hold on! She needs time to lay her egg."

Not knowing how long that was, I held everyone for several minutes. Then I entered the house. Chicken Little was on her nest, no doubt, egg beneath her. I quickly picked up Chicken Little, her nest with its egg, and moved quickly outside. Chicks right behind me. As I emerged from house with my valuable cargo, group applauded, smiles and laughter. They knew my chickens, they understood. As for Liling, you know how she felt.

I went over to our jeep, took the second row bench, Chicken Little immediately sat on the nest with egg that was right beside me. Her 2 chicks standing below on floor board.

"OK, we can go now."

Everyone else had to squeeze in available seats. Liling refused to make eye contact. Mom seemed pleased, supportive. Drivers were anxious to drive before dark.

I cautioned our driver, "Go slow, we have a hen on egg back here."

Down the mountain we went. Chicks would "peep" "peep" whenever we hit a rough spot.

We arrived home and into driveway, pulling up next to house. I told the driver, "Let me be first one out, so I can usher Chicken Little and her nest into the house."

Mom asked, "Where are you going to put her? Not in your room."

"How about against the wall in our dining room?"

"OK, but remember, anymore egg laying must be outside. Chicken Little and her chicks must be outside. Liling and Simuna won't stand for anywhere else."

"No problem. I'll help locate a new nest under our house. That is where it all started."

"Philip! Chicken Little doesn't need help. Probably better that you don't. Chickens have been making nests and laying eggs for 1,000's of years. Besides, I want you to start weaning yourself away from Chicken Little and her chicks.

They've become too tame and dependent on you. This has to end sometime. You now have 4 chickens and none are afraid of people. I'm afraid your chickens will start walking into our neighbors' houses, making themselves at home.

Chicken Little probably will lay a few more eggs. Then her baby chicks will grow into hens, and they too will start laying eggs. I can imagine an exploding chicken population, with our house being home base. Good thing none of our immediate neighbors have dogs. Chickens and dogs, or cats for that matter, will not mix. Our phone will start ringing off the hook."

Soon Chicken Little had her 4th chick, making my flock 5 in all. Taming them was a no brainer. They all copied what Chicken Little did. Outside at feeding time, I would give my call, and they'd all come running.

I would throw feed to them, sometimes broadcasting the feed so I could watch them scramble. I loved walking around the yard so they would follow me. When lying on the grass, the chickens would climb all over me.

I kept tabs on the number. Was still afraid Liling would grab one for our supper. As far as I know while I was in residence she never did. She began to appreciate what my chickens meant to me. Still, she never grew attached to any of them, or so I thought. Sometimes I would see her kick one out of the way as she walked through the house.

As she would often say, "Chickens should be outside or in a pen. They're not pets. They're great in chicken adobo."

Tame chickens present an interesting dilemma. Unafraid of people they would approach a person without warning. People were unaccustomed to a chicken walking up to them. If a person backed away the chicken would keep coming. Remember they liked people, and they were always looking for attention or food. If a person held ground, chicken would walk up to their shoes and would peck. This didn't feel good if barefoot or wearing open toed sandals. Person would turn around, walk away quickly, with chicken in hot pursuit. Sometimes more then one chicken was giving chase.

At day's end we had many a laugh talking about the many ungraceful exits of friends who had come calling. Getting into our house wasn't the problem, it was the leaving. Chickens would be gathered at step base, and after our friend reached flat ground, chickens would converge on them. We'd hear, "get away, stop that," a slow walk, followed by a fast walk, a run, sometimes a scream. Mom would say..."For goodness sake, Philip! Call off your chickens."

University President's In-box

Our neighbors and University Faculty became accustomed to my increasing number of tame chickens. While chickens generally stayed around our yard and would gather around me at feeding time, some would wander off, no telling where they would end up.

One morning Mom received the kind of phone call she'd been dreading.

"Mrs. Bernon (Filipino accent) this is Mata the Secretary of the University President.

One of your son's chickens has laid an egg in the President's mail inbox. The chicken is sitting on the egg and won't let anyone approach the inbox. The President must get to his mail.

Mom interrupted, "I'll send Phil right over."

I rushed over to the Office, to the inbox, picked up chicken and egg, and rushed back to our house.

Mom phoning Mata..."We are so sorry, we sincerely apologize."

Mata..."No problem. Must confess, President and I had the biggest laugh over the inbox. We imagined how this would sound at a faculty meeting, "I couldn't get to this important letter because a chicken was sitting on an egg in my inbox." That is one rare excuse, so far fetched, faculty would have to believe it. Of course, many know about Phil's chickens. Already, President is thinking about how he might use "chicken-in-inbox" excuse for not getting something done in future.

"Mrs. Bernon, this made our day. We can't pass in hall and make eye contact without laughing."

Christmas Tree and Living Tree Ornaments

Perhaps the most interesting part of raising pet chickens was the fact that the cotton and straw base of a Christmas tree was a nesting area made in heaven. My chickens couldn't resist laying eggs under the tree. For several Christmases, where the nests would be was always the question, not if they would be there. Presents placed early under the tree, if they were close to a nest, would be off limits while mother hen was on her egg, if I didn't move her away.

Mom was very creative with her Christmas trees; traditional trees such as Blue Spruce, Fraser Fir were not native to the Philippines and its tropical climate. Bamboo sprigs one year, banana leaves and stalk another. Mom would always wrap the bases with green and red cloth, straw, tassels. Invariably an expectant hen would make a nest in the soft tree underbelly, and would lay an egg. We'd come out in the morning, and there a chicken would be, sitting on her egg.

In effect, we had live Christmas ornaments. Neighbors would visit and were amazed at the scene. Some of the chickens had colorful feathers, and they'd blend in quite nicely with the manger scene and figurines for the holidays. Mom appreciated the Biblical significance of life under the Christmas Tree.

Ping and His Chickens Come Full Circle

Liling was always a concern with the chickens or so I thought.

I tried to keep count of my growing number of chickens so if one turned up missing I could take steps to keep chicken out of the pot.

Liling knew I knew the number. She would see me counting, I wasn't trying to, but this could have been a deterrent.

One day I thought I was one chicken down. Could be this chicken had wandered away, and had yet to make it back. Generally, they all came back. Could have had an accident.

I walked into the kitchen to ask Liling if she had seen the missing chicken. I surprised Liling, and to my surprise, I saw her quickly brushing a chicken off her shoulder. "Get down! What are you doing up here, you naughty chick?'

As chicken scampered away, I looked at Liling and she looked at me. I didn't say anything, I just turned around and left the kitchen, hoping she didn't catch the big smile on my face.

Where Are We? A Look Back

As my focus turned to Chicken Little and her chicks, I lost all interest in war games with my stickmen.

Looking back I now realize how being responsible for an animal, even chickens, teaches you something about yourself. I lost some of my self-centeredness.

Another life lesson was how 1st impressions can cloud, confuse your thinking about someone, even some animal like a chicken. Chicken Little seemed so peaceful, no threat to anyone or anything. And then when spotting a mouse, she turned into a ferocious little dinosaur, exposing a secret life of hers I didn't know existed.

Then there is Liling, who I always felt was a threat as far as Chicken Little and her chicks were concerned. At 1st I had it right; she looked at my chickens as imposters in our little world. Over time she changed her attitude toward them, even growing attached to them. She began to appreciate my connection to my pet chickens.

Meanwhile, life moved on. I recovered from my bout with mono; I went away to join my brother at boarding school.

One summer on returning home from school, I noticed there were no sign of chickens, none at all. I asked Liling, "What happened to my chickens?"

"Your chickens were very attached to you. When you left, they lost their center of gravity.

They returned to being normal chickens, joining other chickens in our neighborhood. I see some around every now and then."

"What about Chicken Little?"

"Come. I'll show you."

I followed Liling into the backyard where I used to play war games. I saw it immediately, a small pile of stones near the back bushes.

"We buried Chicken Little here. I thought you would ask. She died a few months ago from a lung infection chickens sometimes get."

"She was a great Chicken, wasn't she?"

"Yes, a great chicken."

"Liling, what's for supper?"

"Chicken adobo."

"Yum, my favorite dish."

Turn back the clock to 1940 as Told by My Mom, and Dad's 1st hand account of the battle for Tarawa in the South Pacific

I had just been born at the local hospital in Dumaguete, the small town near Silliman University where my father was the Presbyterian minister.

WW II was looming

No question the Japanese were going to invade the Philippines. My parents, their Filipino friends, knew they were coming; they didn't know when, but if would be soon. The Japanese had hop scotched their way from island to island in the South Pacific. The Philippines would be an important acquisition. Pearl Harbor hadn't happened yet (December 7, 1941). Nevertheless, the US naval base in Subic Bay was on alert. Subic Bay is on Luzon

Island where Manila (the Philippine's capital) also is located.

The Navy planned to evacuate us if we wanted. The Navy had been in contact with local authorities. Could we and other American families make it over the mountain to the other side? Coral reefs on our side would make it nearly impossible to get us out safely, as they planned to use a submarine that required deeper water. They were given a date, 2 weeks hence.

My parents carried on their backs what they could. My Dad carefully wrapped and packed his favorite leather bound Bible. My Mom was moved to tears as they left virtually all their belongings behind, not to mention their many Filipino friends.

To their neighbors, they gave away furniture, bedding, kitchen supplies, clothes, art work. Some said..."We'll keep them for you until you return." A sick joke would have gone..."Did you lock the door?":.. as they rushed away from the house, starting off in the dark. They met up with 10 other American families. Jeeps took them up the mountain, road stopped at our current little house where they ate a small supper and spent the night, most on the floor. Filipino military guides would take them the rest of the way on foot. Next morning they ate a quick breakfast and continued the climb up the mountain. My Mom had me swaddled and carried me in front with straps over her shoulders. "Be as quiet as possible, it's best your son doesn't cry." They climbed quickly up and over the mountain, following a narrow, rocky trail. Wet patches, some slipped. Was a relief to start heading down after the climb up. Everyone getting tired from climbing the steeps at a fast pace. We reached the beach in the early morning, still dark. All of us looked out to sea, Mom wasn't sure what she was looking for. "What does a submarine look like in the dark?"

Then she thought her eyes were fooling her, but she saw blinking lights in what seemed a long way out to sea. One of the guides used a flashlight to signal back. The guides pointed out the 4 boats pulled up on the beach. Mom hadn't noticed them before as she was straining to look for something out in the dark water. Good thing the sea was calm. An officer, speaking to the 10 families now exhausted from the hike... "We'll use these motor boats to take you out to the submarine. Get in quickly."

We did that, and the guides staying behind pushed the boats off and away from the sandy beach. Turned around, they motored toward the rendezvous point which seemed far. Mom was very nervous, she had me with her. She said I was quiet the whole way, comfortable in my tight wrap. My Dad sat stoically silent; he was praying.

All of us held our breaths, we could not see anything. A flash of light still in the distance was answered by our driver. Our small boat trip seemed to take forever. Then my Mom saw it, what looked like a large smoke stack sticking out of the water. Then this massive dark structure quietly emerged from the sea. The evacuees gasped. The submarine seemed huge, all of us were looking way up. The wake from the sub almost capsized our boats, water splashed in.

"Hello, the boat," shouted a seaman who flashed a light on a small ladder leading up to the top. Mom thought..."I can't climb that thing." A sailer quickly came down the ladder... "Ma'am, give me your baby." Without thinking Mom held me out, the sailer took me, and quickly climbed up. Mom thought..."I can't believe I did that." The sailer and I were gone, into the bowels of the sub, sleep kept me from crying.

In the pitch black, evacuees began climbing up the narrow, steep ladder. Mom was in no hurry, she waited until nearly everyone else had disappeared up the ladder. Dad said..."Come on Dot. It's your turn. I'll be right behind you." As if in a dream, the climb, then the small deck, the friendly smiles, no one said a word, and immediately into a circular staircase down.

Sub seemed warm and brightly lit. She blinked her eyes. She was amazed how small the sub seemed now that they were inside. They were led along a narrow corridor, pipes on walls and above, to a small room with bunk beds. Then she felt the vibration, heard the rumble of engines. She realized after they were all in the sub, it had slipped quietly under the water, and was running silent and deep. Seemed loud to her, maybe from the vibration.

The sub took them to a Navy transport ship. Mom had to repeat the climb she endured before. Narrow ladder to a low deck, then into the ship. Transporter provided more spacious accommodations.

The ship took a circuitous route to Australia to avoid Japanese subs. A patch of rough seas made them all seasick, but not me. From there another ship took them to New York City where my parents would live until their Philippines' return.

After Pearl Harbor and US's entry into the war, Dad felt obligated to serve, he joined the marines as a chaplain.

Australia was his first post. While there he corresponded daily with Mom. He would write short notes on restaurant menus, placemats. She often received his letters in a bundle.

Early in November, 1943, Mom received a short note from Dad. "I'm going on an assignment for several weeks. I can't tell you when or what. I will write as soon as I can." The tone of this curt note bothered her...nothing to do but wait.

At the end of November 1943 she saw a newspaper headline. "Marine beachhead in Tarawa results in mass US casualties."

"I wonder if Dad was involved in the fighting on Tarawa?"

"I never heard of that place."

Tarawa is a one square mile coral atoll, highest point is 30 feet above sea level, on which the Japanese had built an airfield.

Mom learned a little about the Tarawa battle. It lasted 4 days. Marines finally wrestled away the island from the Japanese, but at great loss of life. In a book about Tarawa, Dad is referred to as the Chaplain.

The Tarawa toll over the 76 hours amounted to 1,700 US personnel killed and 2,100 wounded, making Tarawa one of the most deadly in terms of duration for the marines in the Pacific theater.

Mom stared at the headline,... "That's got to be it. Oh shoot!"

She had heard nothing from Dad or the authorities. Not long after, she began scanning preliminary lists of marines killed or wounded on Tarawa. Dad was not listed.

A few days later Mom received from the Post Office a large stack of Dad's letters. She knew what she had to do, but she couldn't do it alone. She called a close friend, and they kneeled together on the apartment floor, facing the large stack of envelopes. Mom and friend began sorting the envelopes by date. Mom's hands were trembling.

"Before (Tarawa), before, before, before, then AFTER! Dad wrote this letter a week after Tarawa! They found another. Doug must have survived!" She fell backwards onto the floor. Her friend shouted "All right!" They hugged and cried.

Envelopes, letters were scattered around the floor. No reason to read them, Mom had the answer she was looking for. She regained enough composure to read the letter sent the week after Tarawa.

Dad reported he went through Tarawa unscathed at least physically, although he never regained his hearing loss from the noise of battle.

To my knowledge, he never said a word about Tarawa after.

Bulletin from the Headquarters of the Commandant of the 3rd Naval District, Monday, August 14, 1944

Lieutenant Douglas Vernon was the 1st Chaplain ashore at Tarawa. Commissioned by the Navy in January 1943; he served in the Southwest Pacific from May 1943 until March 1944. Douglas Vernon was a regimental chaplain with the 2nd Division and landed on a coral reef 500 yards off the Tarawa beach November 20, 20 minutes after the 1st marines reached the shore. He came through heavy fire unhurt, except for some scratches suffered from crawling under barbed wire. 200 marines from the 2nd Division, including Douglas Vernon, received Presidential Citations and ribbons for bravery and victory at Tarawa.

The Tarawa Battle Based on My Father's Written Account

After graduating from Naval Training School for Chaplains in NYC, Dad was stationed in New Zealand. This assignment lasted several months, then he noticed the unmistakable gathering of Naval ships in a nearby harbor, which indicated they would soon shove off for a yet to be announced battle. A more telling sign was they were issued frog-skin looking uniforms mottled with green, brown, and yellow splotches. Except for fire arms and light battle packs, all other gear was to be stowed and left at the Base Depot.

Then one evening, Dad returned to his cabin to find a note tacked to his door. "You will report aboard Personnel Carrier # 10 early tomorrow morning for duty as Chaplain of the 2nd Battalion of the 8th Marines."

In the Chaplain's prayer book, marriage and funeral services are bound together in that order. Quickly Dad put his services manual to use as 3 couples were married before marines were shipped out. So Dad's initial assignment as Chaplain began, happily, with marriages before going to battle and, sadly, ended with funerals after battle.

Loading of the Naval convoy took 10 days. Dad's ship was packed with gear "beyond belief." On open decks... amphibian tanks, Higgin's boats, life rafts. With the impending battle, Dad circulated around the decks, and he handed out spiritual tracts to 100s of men of diverse faiths. On Dad's dog tag chain he wore a cross and a Mezuzah which is a Hebrew symbol of God.

Finally they learned they were headed to Tarawa in the Gilbert Islands which is 3 degrees north of the equator in the south Pacific. Tarawa is a coral atoll of several islets. The Japanese had built an airfield on the southwest islet. Here the Tarawa battle was fought from Nov 20 - 23 1943.

As the convoy neared Tarawa, Japanese planes came to attack, they were driven off by US planes from the aircraft carrier guarding the convoy.

The Commander let Dad choose when he would go in with the marines, but told Dad that he should not carry a weapon. "It's not tradition for chaplains to carry a weapon. Besides, if it gets so bad we need you to shoot, it will already be too late."

One day before battle, Dad provided pre-battle services. All marines were ordered to shower, put on clean clothes, and have their hair cropped, to reduce risk of infection if wounded. At midnight a substantial breakfast was served. At 3 AM the marines were ordered into the Higgins boats.

At dawn the bombardment of Tarawa began with big guns on destroyers, combined with airplane strafing and bombing. The intense bombing blew off almost all coconut tree tops.

Then the Higgins boats moved toward the beach. When the front doors of the Higgins boats were lowered, marines discovered they were moored on a coral reef 500 yards from shore. Just then a mortar landed in one of the Higgins boats killing and wounding many marines.

The marines jumped into the water, and they made themselves as small as possible as they crawled to the beach, bullets whizzing all around them.

Most of the Japanese defenders had survived the Naval bombardment. They had dig deep trenches in sand which is a great shock absorber. When the beach invasion began the Japanese emerged from their bunkers and fox holes and began firing on the marines who couldn't fight back until they reached the beach.

On the way to the beach, Dad passed an amphibious tank that had been knocked out by enemy fire. He thought, "if a tank couldn't make it in, how could a mere mortal expect to make it in?"

When they finally made it to shore, and the 75 foot wide beach they had to cut through a barbed wire fence. Then they ended up pinned below a 4 foot parapet.

The Japanese were fearless and ferocious fighters. Some Japanese snipers had climbed up and tied themselves to coconut trees. When shot, they hung there and died.

Dad became shell shocked, and he had lost his hearing. In a dream-like state, he walked along the beach and pulled off shirt buttons from dead American and Japanese soldiers. He kept a small box of these buttons on his desk for year as a grim reminder of the Tarawa battle.

Once he collected his wits, he moved around the battle ground, digging fox holes for the wounded, and helping corpsman hold plasma bottles. A marine off to his right shouted, "How do you like this Chaplain?" Dad gave him the thumbs up sign and replied, "This is wonderful!"

In midst of the fighting, Dad noticed a white terrier that had burst out of a Japanese machine gun nest under intense fire. Dad and marines watched in fascination as the little dog raced 300 yards to a pier held by the marines. Marines cheered as the terrier safely made it to the US side. The little pooch was making what looked like a wise choice.

At the close of the 1st day and a lull in fighting, Dad and marines lay low in fox holes and looked back at the beach. They could see dark mounds on the sand and floating objects that Dad could tell were dead soldiers.

The 2nd day involved intense fighting as marines closed in on the heavily defended airfield. They had to fight their way from sand bunker to sand bunker using machine guns, flame throwers, and tanks.

On the 3rd day, Dad joined a Roman Catholic priest in giving burial rites to 50+ marines. Dad helped in carrying bodies to the mass grave.

On the 4th day, Dad and the marines, since they had been involved in the initial Tarawa assault, were relieved and replaced by fresh troops. The battle for Tarawa essentially was over.

One day later Thanksgiving came, and Dad led a prayer service on board the transport ship. In Dad's Thanksgiving prayer, he thanked God for seeing them through Tarawa, for calming their fearful hearts, for remembering their shipmates who fought and died beside them, for assuring their sacrifices were not done in vain, for comforts and safety of their ship, and, lastly, for being able to rest and share in giving thanks.

The End